Wakefield Press

the Dog Rock

Miriel Lenore was born in Boort, Victoria, and was educated there and in Bendigo and Melbourne. She worked as a plant breeder and student counsellor before moving to Fiji where she was involved in education, formal and informal. After twenty-two years there, and a brief period in Sydney, she moved to Adelaide where she still lives.

Miriel Lenore has recently explored the lives of several women in her family's history who emigrated to Australia in the mid-nineteenth century. *drums & bonnets* presented Lizzie, the first of these women and *the Dog Rock* introduces the second, Sarah. The trilogy was completed with *a wild kind of tune* which follows the life of Sarah's daughter, Caroline.

T0363963

Also by Miriel Lenore

Poetry

the Lilac Mountain

sun wind & diesel

travelling alone together:
in the footsteps of Edward John Eyre

drums & bonnets

a wild kind of tune

smoke

Performance

Text of *Masterkey*

with Mary Moore

(adapted from the novel by Masako Togawa)

the Dog Rock

miriel lenore

Wakefield
Press

Wakefield Press
16 Rose Street
Mile End
South Australia 5031
www.wakefieldpress.com.au

First published, 2004
Reprinted 2019

Copyright © Miriel Lenore, 2004

All rights reserved. This book is copyright. Apart from any
fair dealing for the purposes of private study, research,
criticism or review, as permitted under the Copyright Act,
no part may be reproduced without written permission.
Enquiries should be addressed to the publisher.

Designed and typeset by Ryan Paine, Wakefield Press

National Library of Australia Cataloguing-in-publication entry

Lenore, Miriel.
The Dog Rock.

ISBN 978 1 86254 666 0.

1. Lenore, Miriel – Family – Poetry. 2. Jerrawa (N.S.W.) –
Genealogy – Poetry. 3. Dalton (N.S.W.) – Genealogy –
Poetry. I. Title.

A821.3

CORIOLE
McLAREN VALE

Wakefield Press thanks
Coriole Vineyards for
continued support

for
David, Caroline and Libby

Anchored here
in the rise and sink
of life

Lorine Niedecker

Contents

prelude

tracing the genes

after the jam factory fruit-picking
ward-cleaning dish-washing student days
my first real job – agriculture department:
plant breeding section
                    geneticist grade six

no ethical concerns hampered me
a bungling beginner in the new age
                    of genetic modification –
I tried to induce mutations by shaking up
            chromosomes with chemicals

having failed to produce anything of value
                    (read commercial)
I soon left to begin my own breeding plan
where each arriving specimen is priceless

perhaps that early work spurred
                    the pursuit of my clan
the frustrated scientist finding it easier
                    to trace the genes back
than to design them for the future

the photograph

along with my mother's rings, pearls
                and pieces of china
I keep a thin grey booklet:
        Old Tom Brown of Dalton
an 1860's photograph in the front

my burly great-great-grandfather
leans back in a chair, book in his lap
        patch over his right eye
clean-shaven confident expansive

in his dark cravat and three-piece suit
he fills two thirds of the print

compressed against the frame
        a small-boned slender woman
stands beside him in a plain grey dress
        white ruffled cap, unlined face
strong eyebrows and chin
        determined mouth half-smiling
a modest woman yet the work-worn hand
gently touching Tom's arm is protective

so much is told of Tom
        so little of her
only twice the booklet names her
this bridge to all my Sussex generations

flight

how far is my search for my grandmother
a search for my own dream of England
born in Anglophile schooldays?

how shall I see Sussex?
will it be country lanes and hollyhocks
spires and grand churches?

will it be the tidy homes
of the retired masters
of Africa and Hong Kong?

or mean streets
          grey towns
                    acid rain?

can I see only what I expect
or will I be surprised?

the perfidy of records

I'm with Simon de Montfort and the barons
as I walk through the Castle precincts of Lewes
to the Old Maltings where Sussex records are kept
    I expect equal success in my quest

yes, here is my great-great-grandmother:
        Sarah, the child of Joseph and Eliath Turk,
        baptised 22/12/1811 at Hartfield.
a census shows her there in 1821
and ten years later
she marries Tom Brown in the next village
I'm ecstatic
go down to the nearest pub to celebrate

back in Australia I tell our family historian
I'm searching for Tom Brown's wife Sarah
        strange, I've not researched her family.
not so strange I think
he downloads his file:
        Sarah Turk: daughter of Thomas Turk,
        the son of John and Rebecca of Iden.
        Born 18/12/1811 Wednesday Sussex England.

the perfidy of records!
Sarah from Iden with a father named Thomas!
how do you know? I ask
        it's on her death certificate:
        Father's Name, Thomas. No birth village.
        there was a Thomas of the right age in Iden.

I'm devastated
                      I want her to come from Hartfield –
it's pretty, it's on the edge of the primeval wildwood
it's Christopher Robin's place
                      and I found her there

how to counter this Iden thing?
after her death did Sarah's son Elias
give *his* father's name on the form?
easy to do at such a time

another search in Lewes produced no Sarah
born to a Thomas in Iden
or anywhere else in Sussex in December 1811
only Joseph's daughter Sarah fits the date

have I made my case?
I'm staying with Hartfield

the garden of England

the font

the shingled spire of St Mary the Virgin's church
points to the skies above Hartfield
I take a room at the Anchor Inn
and eat a pork pie before
            setting off to hunt for Sarah

up Church Street, through the lych-gate
            below its overhanging cottage
into the graveyard where my relatives must lie
            I hurry towards Sarah's baptismal place

wall plaques in the austere old church
            make no mention of my family
but light through clear windows
falls on the fifteenth century font
with its panels of oak leaves
            flowers and protective shields

here her parents stood as the curate
            signed the cross
praying for blessings on their first-born
            willing health for her
and an easier life than theirs

good luck

December 1811
well-rugged against the cold
my godparents carried me
to St Mary's church for baptism
happy when the cold water
made me cry: a good sign

they made sure my name
was not said before service
nor the water wiped off my head
but my mother wasn't certain
Father had gone to the hive
to tell the bees of my birth

that might explain the bad patches
I've met amongst the good
I keep my fingers crossed

the rector

I assume the curate baptised Sarah
since Lord Acton the Rector of Hartfield
was too exalted to stay in the parish
christening the children of simple folk

Joseph and Eliath Turk lived
with her parents in the house at Pay Gate
far from the corrupting effects of power
a later Lord Acton would expose

a temptation grown-up Sarah
also escaped since a mother knows
how little power she has
so quickly gone and never absolute

the bells of St Mary's

1783 AD

Hartfield Sussex Feby 6 . . .Wednesday the 29th day of January in the middle of a steady peal the Ringers observed a very sudden alteration in one of the bells, and immediately the Man that was ringing the Third Bell cry'd out, the Fifth bell is broke from which notice the Treble Man said stand. After which they turned the Fifth Bell and found her Tongue too Fatal . . .she was obliged to give up her breath.

William Morphen

2000 AD

there's a small wooden practice bell
               over St Mary's porch door
and the ropes are looped against the wall
a notice reads:
Bell Ringers Practice
every Thursday
7 to7.45 pm Be Punctual
a clock ticks its way to eternity

after an early meal on Thursday
I stroll into the porch where the bellringers
               all women
stand under the tower with their ropes
William Morphen would be surprised

the last of the sunlight catches
the heavy ropes as they rise and fall
               against the shadowy walls
ringing the old permutations of Bobs Doubles
the sound is somewhat muffled
               by the floor above us
but the Fifth Bell is *in full breath* with the peal

outside in the warm evening
the bells are tumultuous
I sit on an old tomb
           musing on my ancestors

a handsome man in casuals wanders over
offers without introduction
           a patronising welcome

we discuss the evening and the view
until I say
      you must be the vicar
           how did you know?
      some air of ownership
           is that a compliment? still smug
      not entirely I say
           that's not fair – I was being friendly
he walks off hurt
I'm guilty but unrepentant

above us and around us
           the bells clang and deafen
with those mathematical changes experts adore
the rest of us admire but seldom love

the Forest

my grandparents' house lay
on the road to Ashdown Forest

as a young lass sent to gather
chestnuts and firewood
I was afraid of the giants, devils
and fairies I might meet
I knew from my granny that some
were helpful like the Dobbs
the household fairies
but the Pharisees of the Forest
terrified me

I had to avoid the giant at Gill's Lap
go round the Devil's Bog
and the secret passage that took you
straight through the earth to Australia
(it could have saved me
a long hard journey later on)

I found no fairies in my new home
the old ones couldn't cross the seas
any local sprites were hidden from me

Poohsticks Bridge

Please use the designated route
the B2026 has no paths

the pamphlet directs me south from Hartfield
past the big oak
and up Newton's Hill on the B2110
to turn alongside Hook Farmhouse
                    (but where is Peter Pan?)

my enchanted place is here on gentle slopes
where the wind moves over pastures
tidy farms lean under the hills
and the path follows lines of oak and beech
the church spire defines distance

Sarah knew these farms under this soft wind
she was born in the valley below
in a house still here ten years ago
her relatives lived at Cotchford Farm
before Christopher Robin wandered
into Ashdown Forest to play Poohsticks

Sarah and Christopher have gone
the bridge too – a farmhand's flimsy work
could not withstand a tourist army
but children still throw sticks
under its heavy successor

Pooh Corner

opposite the Honey Pots Olde English Tea Rooms
six Japanese women carry bulging bags from a shop
soft Poohs and Piglets protrude from the plastic
Christopher Robin in wellies printed on the side

in the bedroom I shared with my brother
        quince tree and dust outside the window
our mother read us the Pooh books at night
I still know poems from When We Were Six

beyond my children's rooms
        moonlight fell on coconut palms
and the dark brooding leaves of the *baka*
as we travelled to the Hundred Acre Wood
        for Piglet to gather his haycorns

grapevines and apples surround the house
in the Hills where I read to my grandchildren
of Pooh floating with the clouds
        Tigger jumping in Roo's sandpit

our pleasure was costly
for the growing Christopher
        imagine his school and the army!
no wonder he left The Enchanted Place
to settle quietly in Devon selling books

is it a solace to his spirit
that somewhere in Yokohama
a child may be laughing at Pooh
        or somewhat puzzled?

equation

how to compute
the *equation of days*
is a problem
not only for sundials

is a day strolling
the paths of Sarah's country
equal to one searching for a farm
in the Tithe Apportionment Maps?

what can be added to a day
reading wills in Lewes
to equal time alongside
the Medway at Hartfield?

what magical measure can equate
long hours in a stationary bus
with the time of a lover's kiss
a friend's call
a grandchild's impossible goal

Hartfield to Withyham

it's my favourite walk –
leave the bus near the Haywagon Inn
cross to Hall cottages and the yeoman's house of 1425
turn into a lane alongside the Town Croft and drop down
off the ridge to river flats on the High Weald Trail
cows watch with mild disdain as you edge
                              along a boggy path
to the tiny once navigable Medway

someone from the village may be exercising a dog
sometimes they will be friendly –
Julie who works in the Old People's Home
told of Mrs Fuller and her postcard collection
                just call on her, tell her I sent you

or they may be like the woman
whose huge wolfhound dog bounded along the bank
        is it a cow or a horse? I asked with a smile
she looked at me, called the dog and hurried off

cross the bridge on the Vanguard Way
above brown water heading for Chatham
                              and the North Sea
then enter a majestic avenue – once railway
now part of the muddy Forest Way –
follow the Wealdway to a plain stone bridge
gateway to Withyham *home of the willows*

as the sun continues to shine
you are at one with Wordsworth Keats etc.
now you can visit the parish church
or go left to the Dorset Arms
                              I choose left

the tower

the Dorset Arms is in Sussex because
the Dukes of Dorset and descendants
have owned everything here for eight hundred years

this inn offers shooting lessons and free pens
a notice appeals to parishioners not to trespass
now the earl has closed the knoll path to the church

a gourmet Ploughman's Lunch strengthens me
for the longer route to St Michael's – though
Transportation has ended I want to avoid the earl's rage

rebuilt over six centuries the church looks all of a piece
the reddish stones of its squat tower
all that remain of a day in 1663:

June ye 16th was Wytheham Church burnt down by tempest
of thunder and lightening which came in at the steeple, melted
the bells, and went up to the chancel and there tore the
monument to pieces.

married

we were both working at Withyham
so that's where we married
St Michael and all Angels
two more angels now Tom said
a joke from my wild new husband

a big church with a square tower
very fancy inside
with a huge marble monument
in the chapel
a young boy touching a skull
with parents and twelve children
kneeling all round him
enough to put you off marrying

the paintings around the walls
were old and gloomy
I liked the one of Jesus
washing the disciples' feet
thought it might give
our master an idea
but I shouldn't complain
we got the time off for our wedding

St Michael and all Angels

an important place for my ancestors
but my interest strays to Vita Sackville West:
did she want her ashes here
                    in the Sackville Chapel
away from the garden she created
the places she loved?

freestanding like an altar, the huge central monument
portrays fifteen marble Sackvilles
the chapel's east window shows no Christ
                    but the family genealogy
the walls celebrate no saints but Sackvilles only
Vita and her father among the rest

the famous Fourteenth Century paintings
                    are in safe keeping
replaced by colourful but lifeless copies
I try to imagine Sarah and Tom standing here
to be married by a Sackville curate
relation of a Sackville vicar

I can't know their response to St Michael spearing
                    the dragon above the entrance
delight perhaps at Christian triumph?
I think Vita would have favoured the dragon

full pelt

I fancied Tom when I saw him
tall handsome broad-chested
like the horses pulling heavy carts

earning money somehow –
prize-fighter, labourer, quarryman
but never keeping a job

drunk, he was sometimes violent
but what young men are not?
he was fervent at loving too

I liked his willingness to live full pelt
it cost me my family and the world I knew
to follow his big dreams: he was enough

the leopard's spots

we boys be dragged up
Tom said of the hard times he weathered

born in the iron village of Burwash
where men were tough, drank lots
and a forge still blew in the main street
(his father a billeted soldier)

the family moved to Withyham
next village to Hartfield
his youth owt but gentle
a wild one, a rowdy fighter
he went with brawling boys
to taunt a Wesleyan preacher
stayed to be converted
in an instant like Paul

for years he flipped between
backsliding and repentance
before he steadied
became a revered preacher
a sort of village saint

but that was in another country

the thrill

if my prize-fighting ancestor Tom
once killed a man as family legend suggests
did he know that thrill of killing
            I heard discussed on Lateline?

a man who conditions police to kill
said it was hard work because
            after the midbrain's thrill at survival
horror and nausea follow when the forebrain kicks in

so far I've only killed rabbits
I recall the thrill as success not survival
            rather like sport   was it sport?
I aimed, I hit and after I saw the eyes, felt sick

Old Tom knew fighting's seductive charms:
long after he was *saved* and a powerful preacher
he thought as he passed a champion fighter
            I could easily polish you off

the professor on Lateline said women kill
with the same emotions as men:
pleasure in saving themselves and companions

she didn't say it was sexual pleasure
as soldiers wrote in wartime diaries
            it was like a screw . . .
            the ache as of orgasm

the ledger

I was told in Sunday school
John Wesley saved England
from following the French
into revolution
an achievement
thought to be good

Wesley knew that people
turn to God
(or revolution)
when times are bad
need Him less
when prosperous

for Wesley
turning to God
meant scorning politics
fostering respect
for church and state

he never fought slavery
or child labour
and yet young Tom
the converted sinner
learnt to read and write
changed his own life
and a district
because of Wesley

colonial

as I began a circular walk around Withyham
two couples started the other way
I chose the public footpath
through Earl de la Warr's imposing beeches
past his cricket ground and ornamental lake
to the high ground beyond his forest

I looked at the rolling pastures between
the earl's two great houses
thought of rural life in Sarah's time:
the loss of common lands and ancient rights
the hardship and desperation

the morning walkers climbed the rise
and stopped to talk
I suppose I started it – I usually do
but they were ready to rest
we talked routes and travels and farming
until I said:

> why didn't the peasants revolt?
> why do aristocrats still own it all?

a microsecond changed the mood
one man said I knew nothing about land
nor the value of large estates
Australians he added were culture-less boors
the women were embarrassed
kept smiling as we parted

Mrs Fuller the postcard lady told me that once a year
the countess entertains senior Guiders to lunch

Mayfield

this High Weald village
where Tom and Sarah briefly lived
could win a Best Kept competition
                    if it ever stooped to enter
it doesn't forget it was once the seat
                    of Saint Dunstan

the village sign shows maidens surrounded
                    by chamomile flowers
since its name could mean maidens' field
or the place of mayweed – *stinking chamomile*

the High Street with its Elizabethan
                    and Jacobean houses
runs along a hillside where even
                    the public carpark offers
the loveliest views in England –
perfect curves of slopes and valleys
just the right balance of hedges
                    fields and fallow

the village doesn't encourage tourists:
the post office shop sells
                    cards of Hastings and Rye
the only visible B&B is April Cottage Teas
where I can't have a room because people
                    are coming for afternoon tea

the librarian thinks Yeomans takes guests
                    and the owner says yes

but at present it's filled with Belgians
there are beds in the Elizabethan Middle House
        but I can't afford them

I think I know why Sarah and Tom didn't stay long
and took their child to Buxted for christening
it begins to rain as I wait under the chamomile
        for a bus to somewhere else

battles

I never liked St Dunstan's church
dark and heavy even with flowers
scene of too many battles

first the Devil pushed Dunstan's wooden church
out of its proper line
so the saint had to shoulder it back
then he undid the builders' work
on the new church – threw down at night
the stones they had placed each day

Duncan was an archbishop, Tom a labourer
but both worked with their hands
burly men and musical
their first churches were so simple
both battled hard with the Evil One

the Devil as a beautiful woman tempted Dunstan
until the saint caught her nose with tongs
sent her flying to Tunbridge Wells
(you can see the tongs in Mayfield's Old Palace)

Tom was tempted with Strong Drink and to miss
a Sunday's preaching – God punished him
blinded his eye when his horse ran into a branch

Dunstan struck a rock and water gushed
(the spring is there today)
a skill Tom never learnt
though needed more in New South Wales

Dunstan was made a saint of the church;
with all my husband's faults
God should be just as pleased with him

in the public records office

did Sarah work at Honey's Wood
Knaves Acres or Daisy Croft?

was she milking cows
at Further Brinkhurst or Mockbeggar farm?

I hope she avoided Roughlands Bridletts
Dimgates and The Old Stews

was Tom quarrying stone in the Marlpit
at Fair Oak or at Marlpit Mead?

so much detail yet the High Hareth of the family Bible
is not in tithe maps or topographical

names change over time the assistant says
I expected them constant since Domesday

maidens' field

in spite of its name or because of it
       Mayfield is a village of men –
saints archbishops martyrs and murderers

three flaming crosses each September
       keep the martyrs alive
ghostly highwaymen ride at Pennybridge

smugglers live on in the stories of
       the delightful naughty Kit Jarvis
who later became a Customs man

Mr Hawkes the murderer carried
       his young victim's body
in a wheelbarrow to her father's house

and poor Tom May died through
       tying his nightcap strings too tight
according to his wife

Mr Turk had been a *slave driver* in Jamaica
       now a rich farmer courted by politicians
he priced his vote at one new hat

surely it was at Turk's quarry that Tom swore
       when he hit his thumb
and to his mates' surprise knelt to ask God's forgiveness

apart from queens, women had to be
        very wicked to be noticed:
Alice Casselowe bewitched to death two pigs and an ox

and Mabel Briggs whose ointment Devil's Delight
        would *Make the Olde Younge*
paid with her life for the remedy

vowels

the English can place you after two syllables
most respond with
   what part are you from?
when I say *Adelaide*
   they reply *a lovely city*
have you been?
   no
it is a litany:
   I have an aunt in Sydney
   I was in Perth in '63

some let you know at once
   that you are not worth breath
but others who serve in shops or on trains
and wait with you at bus stops
     can't help enough
give advice you don't need or plainly wrong
but always with wholehearted friendliness

the conversation at the Half Moon Inn
    began with my vowels
not many patrons:
a tattooed truck driver whose toddler played
   under the sign No Children in the Bar
a young woman in riding gear
   and a quiet elderly chap at the far end

we talked of the pub sign
which showed a crescent moon
> *I know I know the barwoman said*
> *it used to have an upside down witch as well*
> *but I said you can't have that Peter*
> *so he painted it out but left the crescent*

we spoke of horses and roads
and of Australia:
the elderly chap told of the kids
sent out during the war
believing they were orphans
thirty years later one came back
and found his parents alive

our friend wasn't sent so far away
only to York
but it seemed the end of the earth
> *I was so homesick*
> *spent hours and hours making a little*
> *perpetual calendar thing for my mother*
> *much later it came back all broken*
> *and the social worker said*
> *your mother's dead –*
> *he could have said*
> *I'm sorry your mother's dead*

> *I never got over it*

we finished our drinks without speaking

the tide

Buxted is monocultural air
        Prasads in the village store
the only bridgehead from that other world

wartime pillboxes still dot this county
        ancient forts line the coast;
house prices are today's front line

on a nearby railway station
        a Sri Lankan man waits
in tweed suit and porkpie hat

carries two umbrellas for his guests.
        the train is cancelled
we have time to talk

in the precise English which sets him apart
        he speaks of his travels
Singapore Airlines serve French champagne

among the cities he knows well
        Sydney is outstanding
he would be happy to live there

Buxted

home of the beech

i

Sarah's bones are not at this place
where weald meets forest
but could there be some emanation?

in the pub Ned Turner tells me
he saw one night an all-white ghost
at Leppins Bridge, his bicycle sent flying
says the cart that carried the plague dead
still causes spills at the highway exit

I wait among the graves under the yew
on top of hills and by the river
but I catch no sense of Sarah

ii

we hurried to be in before dark:
ghosts could appear at crossroads
to frighten villagers returning late
others haunted the woods

we all knew of the witch Nan Tuck
who fled into Tuck's Wood from Rotherfield
some say she hanged herself there
others think she escaped

many saw her ghost in Nan Tuck's Lane
but she never came to me
I like to think she escaped

the church of St Margaret the Queen

when you read that a church is Norman or Saxon
                    you often discover on arrival
that part of the wall under the south window is Saxon
                    the nave is thirteenth century
the tower fifteenth
                    the belfry added in the sixteenth
and then after years of neglect
                    the Victorians arrived with money
to restore the lot in the light of their taste and theology

this Buxted church is different
most of the structure dates from 1250
the altar rails from 1630, when Archbishop Laud
ordered the rails to be so close that dogs
                    couldn't race around the altar

just before Tom and Sarah worshipped here
the Minstrels' Gallery went
                    and a barrel organ was installed
the vicar reported *our quire is got a liddle out of sorts*

new chapels, windows and lights, though
                    the candelabra keep their candles
new pews but I sit in one from Sarah's time

when I stand at the font where
                    they brought their children
I see more clearly why Tom in Australia
was willing to mortgage his farm for a church
can now imagine that Sarah
                    with thirteen children to feed
might have encouraged him

Janet

at the pub they said if you want
local history, talk to Janet
how will I know her?
if you see a car full of junk that's Janet
or try the church Thursday morning

St Margaret's stands alone in the deer park
above the river, a longish walk from the village
a retired colonel in check suit and moustache
polite and distant
opens the heavy wooden door for me
they must have endless visitors

the service is over
the other five worshippers are re-arranging flowers
polishing the brass, tidying up

I walk down the uneven tiled floor
to admire the fine carving on the pulpit
read the rector's notice to himself:
speak with the voice that wakes the dead

the date in the guidebooks is wrong; it's not Jacobean
I turn to see unruly grey hair
bright eyes in a weather-beaten face
no-nonsense cardigan and skirt
this must be Janet

Janet runs her hand over the pulpit's carved pleating
Mrs Enderby's cousin is a London expert
he says 1600
but there's one like this in Lewes dated 1575

did you notice they're not ordinary marguerites?
I hadn't
the four main petals make a cross – Margaret's flower
did you notice the marguerites on the ceiling have straight stems?
I had not
nor had I seen that two of the painted urns on the ceiling
are upside down for a libation

Janet shows me more marguerites on a worm-eaten chest
as old as the church and two small windows honouring
the sainted Margaret
but it's the plebeian Sarah I follow
do you know a place called High Hareth?
          High Hurstwood?
no it's plainly High Hareth in the family Bible

she doesn't know – she'll look into it

I never returned to Buxted
so I still haven't found High Hareth
no doubt Janet has

domestic virtues

i
this Buxted church is one of only two in England
            dedicated to St Margaret the Queen
exemplary and most pious wife and mother

whose exemplary motherhood is shown
            by her three sons becoming
kings of Scotland after she married the King

both dairymaid Sarah and queen Margaret
            majored in the domestic virtues
both knew a travelling life

a stained glass window
            in St Margaret's porch
depicts the saint with marguerites

the weatherworn stone dairymaid
            above the door holds
her tools of trade as decoration

ii
so good to sit in the quiet church
after the heavy work of the farm

the rector said St Margaret was a queen
made saint for her *domestic virtues*
was she better than my granny and mother?

I always smiled to see above the entrance porch
a carving of a dairymaid with churn –
that was my work, *milk servant*, I liked it there

we brought the young ones for baptism to the font
old as the church and plain like us
Stephen first and Harriet, carried here from Mayfield

by James's time the village had moved to the valley
the earl said it spoilt his view
we too were planning to leave milkmaid and queen

on our last walk up the hill for service
the rector bade us Godspeed
the weathervane pointed south

Taxus baccata

a lot older than I be the village elder said
when asked the age of the churchyard yew

for two thousand years it has been symbol
of death and life, gift and warning

Celts worshipped around it
on the gradual slope above the river

to touch the ancient power
the church was built in its shade

though six supports hold its limbs
it could last another century or two

its shattered trunk was healed with coal
so now you can walk into its huge base

more yews flourish on the northern side
where fewer people are buried

since witches and Satan are known to lurk
in the dark away from the sun

under those protecting trees
my brave or foolish ancestors quietly rest

every cloud etc

*Rather than have his home hemmed in by a lot of menial
neighbours, he (Lord Liverpool) wiped the old village off the
map and dispatched the inhabitants elsewhere.*

> *Greville Cooke: A Chronicle of Buxted*

after the village
        was moved
                downhill

to improve
        the view
                from Buxted Park

the railway
        came along
                the valley.

from their
        new homes
                the displaced

villagers
        could just
                step aboard

garlanding

the wassail broke our shackles
the Christmas mummers
(Tipteers to us)
the games to herald and farewell Lent
the Heathfield cuckoo fair
to welcome Spring
when The Old Woman let the bird go free

garlands and boughs on Flowering Day.
the fairs on quarter days
supper at Hopping Time
and Harvest Home when church bells
called us to a monster feast and games

without these festivals
our souls would die of toil

passion

if Sussex is the Garden of England –
though I suspect other counties
also say the same –

then Buxted is the Garden of Sussex
the Horticultural Society
its Order of Merit

some of the gardens are Didcote-neat
with box hedges around
ordered companies of plants

a house with just such a garden
is Anderida
name of the great primeval forest

others are as casual and original
as Christopher Lloyd would wish
or Derek Jarman who liked his gardens shaggy

cottages peer from screens of hollyhocks
next to the sweeping vistas of grand gardens
great trees could remain from the wildwood

no problems here with conversation
even the first cuckoo
is forgotten when the first fritillaries appear

worshipping Flora

There is this to be said about the English people: give them even a
foot or two of earth, and they will grow flowers in it.

J.B. Priestley

if there's no earth, a hanging basket will do
                for multicoloured petunias
alyssum, tiny daisies, dark blue lobelia

Buxted has earth so frenzies of delphiniums
                asters and dahlias explode beside
huge rhododendrons growing like weeds along the lanes

on a windy May morning their offspring in trays and pots
                fill the village Reading Room
(which houses no book) for the Horticultural Society's annual sale

starting before the advertised time experts stand around tables
                talking of successes and sales
a man tells me he exhibits his *big* begonias at six shows a year

women serve on the coffee and Lucky Numbers stalls:
                instead of ferns I buy coffee and take tickets
win two small prizes of wine and china, not I hope my life's ration

I keep the wine, return the cup and saucer
                to the stallholder's dismay
who still offers to drive me to a distant town

gardeners must be the friendliest group in Sussex
                especially when their village church
is embellished with sculpted flowers

no wonder that in tough pioneering Australia
                Sarah from Buxted
was known for her garden

the move

. . . the worst used labouring people on the face of the earth.
Dogs and hogs and horses are treated with more civility,
and as for food and lodging, the labourer would gladly
change with them.

William Cobbett on England in the 1830's

we married the year after
the Captain Swing riots
and the mobbing winter of 1830
with hayricks burnt and people hanged
most of the country in ferment

we couldn't settle, like so many others
had to follow work, wages too low
enclosures ending jobs –
with three children now to feed
life was desperate

even the weather turned on us
a mighty hurricane in November
hurled chimney pots down
Mayfield High Street
then a killing wall of snow
on Christmas Eve

what could we do?
Tom made his decision

in the first year of the young queen
we took the chance to emigrate
Tom's brother Will and family
choosing to come with us

tears outdid the rain
as we left our Sussex family
they couldn't write to me
nor I to them

proper wives

I remember driving from Albury
              to Sylvia's farm to say goodbye:
so miserable as she packs the family's belongings
              for Esperance, three States away

her parents and sisters are here
her friends at golf and church
Red Cross and Guild –
              so different to come back a visitor

          was it a shared decision?
              oh no she is so proud
              we follow where our men go

Sarah had three oceans to cross
              knowing it was forever
I like to think she and Tom discussed the move
I fear it was
          Wife, tomorrow, New South Wales
she had little choice but to follow her husband
as the church follows Christ

and a moment comes
when risking all is the safest thing to do

the photos

       we haven't seen your photos
my loyal friends welcome me back
to the weekly basil chicken
                at Hawkers' Corner

       I have
Ruth rolls her eyes:
       they're all fonts and churches

       fonts? fonts?
Dee frowns
       as in computers?
I know I'm home

I try to explain my selection:
where others see
       churches and fonts
I see my grandmothers
baptised
       married
             bringing their children
only here could I find them

my friends still haven't seen the photos

the voyage

the tide bell

the weather made leaving worse
rain, a cold wind and mud to the axles –
those cheeky New Foresters could be right
saying Sussex women had the longest legs
in England, always pulling them from mud

the cold made us hopeful too: the agent said
the sun shone all the time in New South Wales

that first sight of the Thames – so wide
and the *Duchess of Northumberland* so small
I feared our luggage might topple overboard
as the waterman rowed us to the ship
this is nothing he said
wait till the Channel and Biscay Bay

too late to turn back

on board we were parted from the men
at least we would eat together
but no sharing of night cries or sickness
I was grateful for William's wife, Susannah

the tide bell clanged as we went downstream
as if it wanted us to go

Gravesend

first haven on the Thames after the marshes to the east
people have landed here for millennia or left
or built forts to prevent others landing

I arrive to a massed display of shape-changing cumulus
squadrons of varied greys
over grey water and the flat expanse of Essex

as I head for the river, a surprising bronze Pocahontas
holds out her arms to barges
lining up for the world's second oldest boat race

across the Thames a small boat ties up at Tilbury wharf
where once hospital ships came
invasion fleets prepared and ten-pound migrants left

Gravesend not Tilbury was the port
when the family arrived with their regulation boxes
to be rowed to the waiting *Duchess*

they were in Poseidon's care whose sculpture
guards the Port Authority
a very pregnant sensuous god

his long hair swirls and flows in rhythm
with the sea – a fine image for fearful
trusting migrants whose God travelled with them

headland

jutting into the Channel
North Foreland separates Broadstairs
from Margate –
those magnets for summer trippers
who come in driving rain or fitful sun

a lolly shop with glass jars to the ceiling
a fish and chip cafe with plastic tablecloth
and icecream sundaes in silver bowls
a beach beside a grey and choppy sea –
sufficient paradise

Sarah would have seen it differently:
as the *Duchess* turned into the rougher Channel
most of them were seasick
the surgeon wrote of his cargo

standing in the rain on the grey shore
a striped lolly bag safe under my umbrella
I look out across the waves
                              for a small ship

on board a tough little Sussex woman
sails past me towards my future

no room for grief

Wed 20th Dec (1837)
Blowing fresh the child of William Brown died last night at half past
8 had the tween decks cleaned breakfasted and had the child
interred, dinner at 2 tea at 5 prayers at 8.

Diary of William Ronald, Surgeon Superintendent

our first time on water! how we prayed!

so cramped between decks Tom couldn't stand upright
women in such narrow bunks midships with the children
                the men up forrard away from us
terrible when the seas came up and we below for days
terrible the darkness at night, the crying babies

when we turned into the channel we were afraid
                then queasy then sick:
the constant smell of vomit on our winter clothes
            so few days permitted to wash
waiting a month for fresh clothes from the hold
as the ship sailed south our bowels tightened –
                holding on to England

and then the tropics!
the children with prickly heat, the rationed water
the arguments and dangerous fights –
I was thankful Tom kept from trouble
                until Cape Town!

the deaths were the worst
the ship's routine allowed no room for grief:
when my infant nephew died
poor William was kept up forrard with the men
I did what I could for Susannah
but next morning they still had work before
their little boy was lowered into foreign seas

her moment

in Cape Town Tom was restless
after fourteen weeks on board
cooped up forrard in the tiny ship
rough seas keeping us all below
nothing but crying children
when the men came back for meals

no space for an outdoor man
a strapping tall prize-fighter
but Cape Town –
blue skies, warm days, long streets
plenty of pubs –
and he wasn't always steady
even after he gave himself to God

no surprise to learn
he was in a police cell
drunk and riotous

the ship about to leave
no chance to disembark –
the children kept on board
as hostages

I hurried to the police
(a thornbill to their eagles)
argued begged and pleaded
yes, me, homebody Sarah
till the officers relented and
gave my husband back

on our walk to the ship
words tumbled from Tom
always penitent
I looked ahead
said nothing

six Kentish cherry trees

harbour

how we kept looking for land!
those last weeks after Cape Town
       were endless
the children crabbier than ever
always someone sick

at least we had proper food
and a clean ship –
       the surgeon's pay
depending on our safe arrival
a man with the power to punish
his decisions not always fair

at last we saw the coast of our new land
and after twenty-two weeks at sea
sailed past red cliffs
       not white
into the quiet waters we longed for

our family of five were all well
as we stepped onto dry land
on the seventh anniversary
       of our wedding day

the small rest

graveyards are full of women
who died in labour
but I've survived
thirteen live births

I did what women are born to do:
every two years
a new soul for the Lord
except when twenty-two weeks at sea
delivered the longest break
between births –
three years four months
in twenty-seven years

Sophie was born nine months
after that first night on dry land

midnight storm

And are we yet alive
And see each other's face?

Charles Wesley

those Parramatta Methodists
living close to hardship and death
welcomed us with the rousing
Wesley hymns we loved

Tom decided we'd get work
at the Cowpastures, those rich river
flats where the Cape cattle multiplied
after escaping from the First Fleet

the move unsettled Tom
he fell quite away
captive again to strong drink
(though always miserable at his fall)

a midnight thunderstorm
struck him back to God
he vowed he'd never again forsake the Lord
and I could breathe once more

history

we always take photos of the wrong place

        not always, Ruth says
        you are too black and white

well often
look we have hundreds of prints
of Camden aerodrome
where we thought Sarah had lived

        not hundreds

well who wants dozens of views
of a windswept field
with no relation to Sarah's story?

        they could make a point

about preparing? research?

        or that nothing is wasted
        as Jeremiah once said
        a quote Sarah would have recognised

        you could write a poem that Sarah might once
        have crossed this bridge and these flats
        scavenging pumpkins from the flooded river
        helping a woman in childbirth
        or going to endless services in chapel
        imagine   create

I'm writing a history

        yes

Cobbitty

in 1809 James Meehan wrote
the indigenous name as Coppety

by 1812 Blaxland called it Cobbotty
as he grabbed a large slice

Macquarie wrote of the Kobbatty hills
Thomas Hassell used Cobbedee

in the 1840s when Sarah and Tom worked
on Hassell's land Cobbitty was preferred

at least they kept the indigenous name
Benhenie vanished into Camden

a rose etc

is it a black-chinned honeyeater
or merely a white-naped?
which species of eucalypt?
where is my grandparents' house?

why this passion to name
to recognise, to place?

I have spent hours
bent over old records
to find whether my ancestors
worked on the properties
of Matavai or Denbigh
wanting it to be Matavai
a link to my South Pacific past

if everything has a place
          so might I

the cure

Lord have mercy upon us for his Reverence has none, a
prisoner is reported to have prayed.
  James Colwell: Illustrated History of Methodism, 1812–55.

plenty of gossip at Cobbitty
about the recently dead chaplain
the Reverend Samuel Marsden

called to help a man with an intemperate wife
Marsden lectured then horsewhipped her
it cured her forever

farmers thought the chaplain a good man
not all wives agreed
the Lord kept me temperate

prayer & work

With the coming of Mr and Mrs Thomas Brown and family . . . the forces of rectitude and righteousness in this country received powerful reinforcement.

(Rev Leslie Taylor)

from the first Tom was busy
badgering people to the Lord
muscular Christianity they called it
loved him in spite of (or for) his
mangling of the spoken word

Camden and Cobbitty became
hot-beds of old-fashioned Methodism
chapels and camp meetings asked for Tom
in our circle he was famous, seldom home

don't misunderstand –
I'm on the Lord's side too
after all He changed
a drunken prize-fighter
into a praying man
I'm grateful, even proud

the Lord gave me plenty to do
four more children born here
nine mouths to feed, at times
with pumpkins only

I was pleased Tom was known as
Mighty in Prayer but
I trust the Lord also noticed me

spreading the Word

In the late 1830s a gathering of unusually talented laymen in the Cobbitty area included . . . Tom Brown.

D. Wright and E. Clancy: The Methodists, A History

the year before we came to Cobbitty
English Methodists sent parsons
so that the poor inhabitants of NSW *be not
consigned to the destructive effects of Popery.*

we only needed them for baptisms
funerals and marriages
we had our own strong preachers
Tom among them, tender and terrible
in the pulpit, shaking his brimstone bag

weekdays and Sundays
we sang and prayed our faith:
our *little Hill of Zion watered
with showers of heavenly blessings*

gradually the Lord led our congregation
to new paddocks in His vineyard
some went north, some west
William's family came south with us
to the hills beyond Goulburn
to Jerrawa

the honey tree

Eucalyptus melliodora: the Yellow Box
well covered and fragrant with honey
what more could you ask for an image of home?
                    Sarah's great-granddaughter

I was camped at Stoney Holes
when David our eighth child was born
while Tom rode off to find a place to buy
now the law encouraged closer settlement

he explored Lord's holding on the Jerrawa
chose land in the arc of Oolong Creek
the hill we called Dog Rock to the south
a Yellow Box on the rise to the north

I think this Yellow Box chose the farm for Tom
so wide and promising shelter
where the land slopes down to the creek

perhaps the name helped –
once Lord's, now it would be the Lord's
Tom spread his large coloured handkerchief
on the ground beneath the tree
and thanked God for his blessings

I came with the children in the wagon
didn't care where he chose
just wanted to stop in one place

we built a slab hut on the flat
near the wide Box tree
I stayed fifty-five years
under its protection

that tree became our church
for camp meetings, prayer meetings
christenings, Sunday services
sweet as honey to Old Tom
sweet enough for me

anniversary 1985

a hundred and fifty years
after the church was built
the gathering worshipped
under the old Box Tree

a giant when they came
today it would still shade
a couple of cricket pitches
if there were enough people to play

some of the branches look tired
but the honey is still flowing
the family planted seeds
and the saplings are doing well

the Dalton fossils

Early in the 1880's . . .Baron Von Ettingshausen dated the
(fossil) leaves as up to 55 million years old because he saw
similarities to European and Arctic plants. Now 21 million
years is suggested

J. Boddington

the casts are perfect
you would swear the leaves are lying on the rock
the veins so clear, so delicately interconnected

yet this leaf with the broken point, the crenulated edge
has been here for twenty million years
since lava flows dammed the Lachlan
and Dalton was a lake

studying the fossils in the British Museum
Ettinghausen saw only what he expected

and the Ngunnawal who watched my ancestor
         mark out his selection on their land
who cared for this country over millennia
who are absent from my family's story

they too were being studied, measured, dated
         their bodies sent to Europe's great museums
in the sunset of their dying race
an expectation as wrong as the botanist's
         a tragedy of a different order

cultivators

sun hot on my back
I am turning the soil
beside our new hut
my hoe the first ever
to break the surface

exiled from Paradise
(though ours was nearer Hell)
I could be Eve planting seeds
to make another Eden

Tom's small plough rips the earth
ready for wheat
these first crops will be heavy
if the rains come

later we'll plant
English willows
by the creek
there's plenty of water

we have named the farm
Dog Rock after the hill
where Tom sat out all night
to shoot the dingoes

the Dog Rock

not craggy   not majestic
not gentle   not Sussex
this hill rising from the creek
walls in the farm from southern gales

sunlit or brooding
or heightened by snow
its boulders defy easy approach
once sheltered dingoes

the hut faced the other way

for fifty-five years Dog Rock was
the disturbing backdrop
to Sarah's days in orchard
garden, cowyard

for the next hundred
a comforting view
from her sons' front verandas

lovers climbed here
families picnicked
exorcisms happened
and healing, if you stayed
long enough with the rocks

the years have muffled
the sound of dingoes and gun

the hut

we quickly built
our first hut
on flat land near
the creek named Oolong
for the brolgas

wide slabs of Box for walls
Stringybark for thatch
chimney of stones and pug
the earth for floor

from the door
I could see brolgas dancing

memorial

after lunch with my mother's cousin
we walk past his hangar and plane
the extensive sheep yards
shearing sheds smelling of lanoline

to the ramshackle hut of two rooms
and a veranda about to fall
that Sarah's grandson Jabez built

in the centre of the kitchen
a table stands unchanged
on its square slab of earth
inches above the ground

here his wife Florrie each day
swept those vanished layers of soil
the stranded table
her memorial

bread & roses

hardest of workers
those settler women –
heavy pots on the open fire
soap and candles to set in their moulds
back-breaking laundry in heavy tubs
sweeping, cooking, making clothes
so many children underfoot

yet always the hours of labour
to soften the harsh beginnings
papers pasted to walls
to warm and beautify the tiny hut
cheap curtains to enclose a bedroom space

and their gardens:
the essential vegetables and fruit
but always, always the straggling flowers
watered with slops – geranium
pigface and where possible
a hedge to keep the wideness out

six Kentish cherry trees

Grandfather and Granny were very energetic people.
Whatever they undertook, it was well and truly done.

their granddaughter Maria
described Dog Rock garden
so clearly you could draw a plan:

six Kentish cherry trees
            outside the sweet briar hedge
on the north side of the house

hops in the orchard to the east
            like those they grew in Sussex
and more cherries, apple, pear and peach
            gooseberries and quince

a hedge of yellow furze and plum
            corrals flowers to west and south:
the perfume of honeysuckle
            moss roses, white and red

the prolific flowers of elderberry
            promise a later wine
surely somewhere a rosemary bush
            for remembrance

it could be a Sussex garden
set among paddocks and gum trees

the Lord's Work

Wife lift up for me
Tom always asked for my prayers
as he climbed into the saddle
to ride off on the Lord's business
up to three days in a week
not
sorry to leave you with the children
sorry you'll have to watch the sick calf
pick the gooseberries
cart more water
not
sorry I can't help you
or
Wife I'll lift up for you

sometimes my devotion
to the Lord
is not as strong as Tom's

revival

Tom and the other preachers
led the district in a great revival
sweeping like a grass fire
through Wesley Vale and Jerrawa

even wild thieves and drunkards
we thought unreachable
converted to the Lord
became *pillars of rectitude*

only the bushrangers
the Lachlan men
hiding in steep gullies
refused to heed the call.

though our husbands
had a soft spot
for these lawless men
we wives were a little afraid

and when Hall's gang
shot a local policeman
all goodwill towards them
was gone

to prevent murmours

Jerrawa – The Government Surveyor and staff have just
completed marking out a township on Oolong Creek in the
County of King, which it is proposed to call Wesley Town as
there are so many of the Wesleyan persuasion in the district.
                          Sydney Morning Herald 22 July 1861

what a to-do over naming!
it had always been Wesley Vale

we saw no good reason to change
but the other Christians did

to prevent murmours and complainings
they suggested Jerrawa the district name

no one knows why Dalton was chosen
it could be for an English lord

at least Jerrawa Creek kept its name:
running water – may it stay true

though amongst the first here
we never bought a block in town

Dog Rock was enough for us on earth
and we hoped for a mansion in heaven

no garlanding

so little came with us:
the Christmas goose
the pancakes, hot cross buns
and Easter eggs
Plum Heavy Pudding and syllabub
but no drink of Huckle my Bluff
and not the garlanding

bells at harvest called us
to church not games
and quarterly *love feasts*
instead of fairs must do
for Wesleyans like us

too busy to mourn lost festivals
we began new gala days:
a feast for every chapel opening
baptisms and weddings brought
our far-flung clan together
and sparsely settled districts
had to become our villages

a vote of thanks to the ladies

1855 Wesley Vale
At the opening of the first chapel 150 persons did
*ample justice to the good things which had been
gratuitously provided by the ladies*

1858
After Mr Thomas Brown laid the foundation
stone of the new brick chapel in the presence of
300 persons, the *assemblage then adjourned
to the luncheon which was an excellent and
ample affair*

1860
A surprising crowd came in bad weather to
the opening of the new chapel and enjoyed
an ample repast

1999
on a cold sunny morning outside the chapel
I meet other descendants of Tom and Sarah
find I'm related to all the congregation bar one

the simple light-filled building
has flowers and plants on every surface
other women help Phyl on roster –
she has no time to garden now Les is ill

all ten of us, nine women and one man
spread to the heaters
the organist, my relative twice over
in her mid-eighties, deaf and almost blind
knows the tunes by heart

we sing as lustily as a scattered dozen can
hear the woman minister preach a sermon
on Babette's Feast, an instance of grace –
the extravagant, unexpected, unrecognised gift

later I ask the organist about our ancestors
she doesn't remember
it's too far away Phyl says
taking me home for an excellent and ample lunch

the zeal of Thy House

*"Be there before time if you wish to get a seat, or you will have
to stand, . . . Friend Brown raises the tune, and all sing, and
they do sing . . . the preacher will hear plenty of Amens and
Hallelujahs and 'Glory to God', and souls are saved . . .*

The Reverend J. Watkin June 1858

our Chapel Opening was delayed:
no one would cut shingles at harvest
so the builder went elsewhere
we wouldn't have chosen winter
with days of heavy rain
flooded creeks and cold winds
we were surprised so many people came

still everyone was happy
the reporter from Yass so impressed –
*a neat brick structure
the walls twenty feet high in the clear,
neatly ceiled with cedar
and the pulpit and communion rail
are very neat and tasty.*

so little debt remaining
the bigwigs praised our efforts
begged us to *finish it today*.
I sat up at Tom's promise to raise
money for the Mundoonan chapel
when ours was paid off

when he offered, *though a poor man*
to sell a farm if that would clear the deficit
I thought of our eight sons needing land
and crumpled
I sinfully prayed that the giving
be not too generous

I don't know if the Lord listened
but for now, our boys will have their farms

the brethren

when Tom needed a horse
for his preaching appointment
he went to James Bush's place

James was not at home
so Tom, busy servant of the Lord
took the horse anyway

James was so furious
he left our church built another
on his land at Greendale

people said the Primitives got to him
but I think Tom was the trouble
not for the first time

Tom's axe, Sarah's fig tree

i   one hundred and fifty years later
Tom's axe is now in the church

where he prayed and preached
would have mortgaged his farm to build

a glass case at the front
alongside pulpit and Table

keeps the axe as relic
like a saint's body in Rome

great-grandsons found it under wheat
where the old slab hut once stood

unsettling to hold it in my hand
this axe which felled the box trees

silted the creek
fed his flock

                              ii   the fig has lost all shape
                                    all modesty
                                    twigs and branches push past
                                    circumference
                                    a wild matt reaching to the sky
                                    like an Irian headdress turning
                                    humans into gods

                                    no leaves on this wild spirit
                                    no singing birds
                                    yet small green buds push out
                                    through toughened twigs
                                    I break one off and keep it

blessings

we needed a name
for our thirteenth child

after the New Testament gave us
Stephen, James and Thomas
we turned to the Old

first David then for our ninth –
Benjamin, hoping that like Jacob's son
he might be our last

the Lord had other plans
He sent three more –
Mary, Elias, Ebenezer

the four eldest left to marry
but eight still crammed
into the tiny cottage to welcome
the baby we called Job

not to wish on him Job's suffering
just strength enough to argue
for his life with God
perhaps he did – he lived
and the Lord sent no more

very boring

the ethologist on TV
says female elephants
have thirty calls
for their children
and one mating call

the male elephant
has only one call
for its entire life
which the scientist
translates as
who's on heat?

very boring he says

Sarah and her four daughters
might think humans similar:
fifty-six children between them
in a few short years

not much time for conversation
or was their husbands'
Praise the Lord
an advance?

the Lord giveth

1861 the bleakest year!

as winter was ending my darling
Mary just nine-years-old
died of *the pneumonic plague*

before buds opened on the cherry trees
David followed and ten days later
Ebenezer the four-year-old

and they were not frail babes –
David at fourteen was almost a man
my helper with hoe and axe

he was the travelling child
born in the Stoney Holes tent
now travelled on Home

I know our children were only
borrowed from the Lord
are now *safe in the arms of Jesus*

but three taken in twenty-six days
too heavy a blow

the widow

Well wife, I leave you in the hands of the Lord.

at sixty I'm a widow
with all Tom's estate and effects
providing I stay that way –
I agree – you can't have family
wealth given to another man

I'm not likely to be tempted:
too busy
with three boys still at home
though Benjamin will marry soon

Elias and Job are good boys
hard workers on the farm
and nearby sons help when possible
but the house and garden
orchard, hens and cow are still my tasks

I make the candles and soap
bread, butter, jams and pickles
preserve the meat, fruit, vegetables
deal with the clothes

I miss Tom and his cheerful faith
but he knew I would be safe in God's hands

1887

what mother can bear
her lovely daughter's madness?

she was always so calm
Caroline my middle child
my special helper when her sisters left
most needed when the children died

married at eighteen and soon a settler
she was too busy for visits home
twelve children in just seventeen years
(I took twenty-seven summers for mine)
did all those pregnancies break her?

does grief cause madness?
son, father, husband, friend all dead
the new husband at war with her sons
too fond of her daughter

was it melancholia after the last birth
soon racing to dementia in the asylum?

could I have helped?
should I have gone to her?

do I dare call this God's will?
I only know that Caroline is lost to me;
in this life I will never see her again

another winter

Mary, David, Ebenezer
Tom and Sophia all dead
Caroline locked away in Gladesville
enough to bear

now Benjamin –
committed to an asylum
within weeks
gone to Heaven

too young at thirty-eight to leave
seven children and a pregnant wife
what went wrong I wonder
he was a worrier
perhaps the debt on his new house
proved the last straw

if I look from my veranda
towards Benjamin's farm
I can almost see him coming
under the Box tree

I must remember God is merciful

Dog Rock Farm

four generations of homes have grown here:

nearest the creek
the slab hut with bark roof and later shingles
dirt floor and a fireplace of stones and pug

then the cottage of three rooms with
sleepout and veranda of slabs, a wooden floor
roof still of shingles but the chimney is brick

Tom called this house *the Mansion*
kept the first hut for his noisy
private talks with God

at some time in the next century
a substantial timber house is built on the slope
facing away from earlier avatars

later still a smaller modern bungalow
housing the latest generation
is closer to the creek again

today there is no Dog Rock Farm
the signs on the gate now read
Ferndale, Sunnyside, Oak Retreat

continuity is in the freedom to name your house
in the memorial on the site of the hut
the Yellow Box seedlings along the drive

and the great-great-great-granddaughter
                named Sarah
who lives on the farm today

old age

I'm never alone at night
often Grace Brown stays here
or my grandson Norman sleeps
in the little room off the veranda
lights the morning fire, chops wood
and brings the water

the day is mine alone
to garden as much as I can
and to keep the house respectable

though dead thirty years Tom is never far away
I sleep in the old bed where he died, saying
this morning I am in the land of Beulah

still my children are around me
I can see young Tom's house from here
James' land is north of Ben's
Stephen my gentle first-born
farms the other side of Dog Rock hill
and Sarah lives next door to him
Elias and Job are near the cherries
grandchildren come most days –
and the Box tree blossoms for the bees

I like sitting on the veranda
comfortable in my rocking chair
wrapped snug in my shawl
thinking of family here and over there

I wish I could write to them
too busy to learn
but if I close my eyes I can see it all:
Hartfield spire above the Medway
and my Granny's Pay Gate home
Ashdown Forest and the stone dairymaid
at Buxted that I used to pretend was me

I smile at the worn antimacassar
on the back of the chair
it has a hole in the shape of Australia

devilish

why has no one mentioned
        her eyebrows – the most startling
feature in her ageing face?

they recall dark mountain peaks
        points of ancient spears
the circumflex that makes an emphasis

do they hint that under the tranquil face
        she showed the world
something lurked untamed and devilish?

did anyone know this Sussex girl
        this Dog Rock matriarch
this ancestor to thousands?

in her last photo she looks away
        from us to a far place
I have to leave her there

the door

all that is left of the cottage
        they called The Old Home
is a simple door of wooden planks
that Sarah's great-grandson
        carted up the slope
to use in his new shed

I lift the metal latch
        and walk through
hoping to catch the shadow
of the woman who
for more than fifty years
opened this door to cross
between
garden and house
light and shade
summer heat and coolness under thatch
winter winds and fireside warmth
solitude and crowding
        – the woman who
        was finally carried through

no English estate

Les can't walk far on his damaged feet
$\qquad$ his blood is slowing
so he stays in his house on the rise above
the site of his great-grandparents' first hut

he has fought in a war
known generosity from a man not kin
and malice from one who should be close
worked hard on a block too small
yet his welcoming eyes, direct and innocent,
surprise me and humble –
$\qquad$ here is a man without guile

as I sit in Sarah's restored rocking chair
he shows me her will signed with a hesitant cross
this woman who gave us both some sturdy genes
who, like Les, was steadfast
$\qquad$ as the boulders on Dog Rock hill

from his window he sees the hill
where Old Tom shot the marauding dingoes
the mulberry tree Sarah planted on the flat
$\qquad$ the willows along the creek
it's not flowing as fast or wide as they knew
$\qquad$ but still can flood after snow

the original block is shrinking
$\qquad$ divided at each generation –

this is no English estate where the firstborn son
inherits all – not here thank you!

Les can still see his son's wheat
on the flats, his cattle on the slopes

an era will end when
no descendant of Sarah farms at Dog Rock

judgments

the graveyard plot
has to be large – it holds
the big bones of Old Tom
       those of tiny Sarah
and their three young children

a broken headstone lies
across the new cement grave:
       Sacred to
the Memory of Sarah Brown
also Thomas Brown
also David, Mary and Ebenezer

what else could we do with it?
       my relatives ask

the new headstone
has changed the order:
Tom's name is now first
       Sarah is the also

I must acknowledge
Tom was the busy preacher
       and public figure
but who sits
on their Father's right hand
       is less certain

those Turks

since the 17th Century, those stones in the forecourts of Wiltshire Barrows
or in the Megalithic circles at Avebury have been known as sarsens
meaning Saracens meaning strangers meaning nomads
meaning eastern meaning sunrise
meaning Turk

hard sandstone boulders lying on the chalk downs
lifted into monuments 5000 years ago
were also known as Bridestones
meaning the goddess Brigid
meaning beginnings
meaning fertility
and seasons
endings

these massive shapes evoke for me
a tiny Sussex dairywoman
Sarah Turk

who knew hard nomad years, hard settler years
& what it was to be a stranger in a new land
thirteen children proof of her fertility
and the long years of gardens
what monuments for her?
a broken headstone
some dying trees
and a pillar on
the site of
her slab
hut

Chronology

born 18 December 1811
at Hartfield, Sussex
to Joseph Turk and Elizabeth Sendall
married Thomas Brown
at Withyham, Sussex
on 26 April 1831

they lived at High Hareth, Mayfield and Buxted
before sailing with three children from Gravesend
on 14 November 1837
in the Duchess of Northumberland

they arrived in Sydney on 22 April 1838
settled for some years at the Cowpastures
(as Camden and Cobbitty were first known)
where four more children were born

another child was born in 1846 at Stoney Holes near Gunning
in 1847 they moved to Dog Rock Farm at Dalton
where five more children were born

within four weeks in 1861
three children died

Old Tom died at Dog Rock Farm
on 16 February 1871 aged 59

Sarah died at Dog Rock Farm
on 26 September 1902 aged 90

a great-great-great-granddaughter, Sarah,
lives at the farm today

Acknowledgments

I am indebted to my relatives at Dalton, especially Colin and Phyllis Brown and Phyl and the late Les Brown, for hospitality in welcoming me to Dog Rock and for generously recounting family stories. Brian Riley was also generous in sharing family records and in providing the stories of Cape Town and the supposed killing. The interpretation of Sarah's life is my own.

I am grateful to ArtsSA for grants enabling me to visit the places in New South Wales and Sussex important to Sarah Turk, and to Jayne Jennifer and Gillian Gray for giving me a base in London. Fellowships at Varuna and Booranga Writers' Centres provided the perfect writing environment, as did my cousin Helen Heathcote's beach house.

The librarians and Records Office staff I met in London, Sussex, Sydney and Canberra were unfailingly helpful in my hunt for Sarah and her world. Books by Ed Hazell, Rosalie Bush and Dorothy Pirchan gave me a picture of Jerrawa, in southern New South Wales, and early histories of Methodism in that State provided information on Thomas Brown.

Friends and colleagues including Kaz Eaton, Diane Fahey, Jill Golden, Annette Marner, Margaret Merrilees, Kay Schaffer, and Marie Tulip have been generous with their insights and support. Susan Hampton's advice has been invaluable and, as always, Ruth Raintree has given more than anyone could ask.

Some of these poems have been published in *Overland*, *Poetrix*, *Social Alternatives*, *New England Review* and *fourW*, and read on Radio Adelaide.

Wakefield Press is an independent publishing and
distribution company based in Adelaide, South Australia.
We love good stories and publish beautiful books.
To see our full range of books, please visit our website at
www.wakefieldpress.com.au
where all titles are available for purchase.
To keep up with our latest releases, news and events,
subscribe to our monthly newsletter.

Find us!

Facebook: www.facebook.com/wakefield.press
Twitter: www.twitter.com/wakefieldpress
Instagram: www.instagram.com/wakefieldpress

Printed in Australia
AUHW010404010419
310479AU00003B/8

9 781862 546660